T0159474

# BORGES IN 90 MINUTES

# Borges

## IN 90 MINUTES

Paul Strathern

IVAN R. DEE

CHICAGO

BORGES IN 90 MINUTES. Copyright © 2006 by Paul Strathern. All rights reserved, including the right to reproduce this book or portions thereof in any form. For information, address: Ivan R. Dee, Publisher, 1332 North Halsted Street, Chicago 60622. Manufactured in the United States of America and printed on acid-free paper.

www.ivanrdee.com

Library of Congress Cataloging-in-Publication Data:
Strathern, Paul, 1940–
    Borges in 90 minutes / Paul Strathern.
      p. cm. — (Great writers in 90 minutes)
    Includes index.
    ISBN-13: 978-1-56663-695-7 (cloth : alk. paper)
    ISBN-10: 1-56663-695-7 (cloth : alk. paper)
    ISBN-13: 978-1-56663-694-0 (pbk. : alk. paper)
    ISBN-10: 1-56663-694-9 (pbk. : alk. paper)
    1. Borges, Jorge Luis, 1899–1986.  I. Title.
PQ7797.B635Z9185  2006
868'.6209—dc22

                                        2006022192

# Contents

# BORGES IN 90 MINUTES

# Introduction

Borges was a man of immense learning, yet by one of those ironies in which his work abounds, his life came to resemble a simple primitive fable. The more he learned and wrote, the more his sight failed, until in the end he became totally blind, lost in the world of his own mythological stories.

Borges had always been a bookish man, deriving an unusually high measure of his inspiration from the library rather than from life, but his gradual loss of sight played an increasing role in his work. As his sight faded, and the streets of Buenos Aires around him withdrew into "a pale uncertain ash-grey," so his inner vision tended to turn away from the South America into which he had been born, and gaze longingly toward the Europe of his ancestors. Symptomatic of this was his change of allegiances. Early in his career he had been influenced by the almost surreal fecundity of the great Nicaraguan poet Ruben Dario:

> The shaggy crabs, like roses, all have thorns,
> and the molluscs, reminiscences of women.
> Learn to be what you are, embodied enigmas,
> And leave the responsibility to the Norms.

Later, Borges would turn to the more austere European vision of Franz Kafka:

> One morning Gregor Samsa woke from a night of troubled dreams to find himself transformed into a gigantic insect. He was lying on his hard armor-plated back, and when he lifted his head, he saw . . . his many legs, pitifully thin compared with the rest of his large body, were waving helplessly.

In a similarly horrific metamorphosis, Borges would wake up blind. The life of the outside world, which he so little regarded at the best of times, was taken away from him. Instead of life and light, he was reduced to darkness and learning.

Such suffering and aridity would have overwhelmed any normal man, but Borges was far from normal. He retained, throughout his life, a naive, almost childish element at the heart of his character, and the poetry that came from this innocent source breathed life into the dry, bookish desert from which he drew his inspiration. The desert blooms he created were short, much as real desert blooms are short-lived, but they were also strange and weirdly exotic. Amidst the cactus spines of scholarship sprouted petals of piercing beauty. His work had an uncanny knack of being both profound and poignant, timeless yet touching—a product of deep suffering and incorrigible innocence.

On the other hand, this innocence, and its accompanying timidity, marred his life. Sexually and emotionally, existence was for the most part a catastrophe for this mother's boy, who remained unmarried until he was well into his sixties. And not through choice: he was constantly falling in love, but the women simply didn't find him sexually attractive. When he finally married at sixty-eight, even this didn't work out. So he went back to mother. But as he was forced to admit to himself, the "I" who lived his life was gradually overshadowed by the "Borges" who wrote, whose words would bring him his only lasting solace.

# Borges' Life and Works

Jorge Luis Borges was born in Buenos Aires, the capital of Argentina, in August 1899. By the turn of the twentieth century, Buenos Aires was already a city of considerable wealth and sophistication, more so than many capital cities in Europe, and was regarded as the cultural center of South America. Borges was born into a distinguished family whose ancestors included an Argentine cavalry officer who played a leading role in the country's nineteenth-century struggle for independence from Spain. Another branch of the family was British, and Borges learned to speak English before he spoke Spanish, acquiring the nickname "Georgie," an English version of his name. His father was a lawyer with frustrated literary ambitions who also took up as a part-time teacher of psychology at a prestigious English-language girls' school in the city. His extensive library was filled with works by mainly English-language writers such as Robert Louis Stevenson, H. G. Wells, and Mark Twain, all of which would later be eagerly absorbed by the precocious young Borges.

Despite the family's middle-class status, their home was in Palermo, then a run-down suburb on the northern outskirts of the city, whose dives and cheap nightclubs were notorious for tango-dancing (then considered highly unrespectable) and lethal knife fights among the Italian immigrants and indigenous lowlifes. Later in his life Borges would find himself mentally drawn to investigate this forbidden territory.

Although Borges' father was something of a womanizer in the accepted traditional manner of the period, life at home was largely happy, and young Georgie developed a close relationship with his mother, his sister Norah, and his English grandmother. Borges' mother would often take young Georgie to the nearby Palermo zoo, where he developed a curious obsession with a tiger. He would insist upon standing before its cage until sunset, when the zoo closed, and one of his earliest creations was a childish drawing of this tiger, dating from when he was just four years old. Until the age of nine, Georgie was educated at home. Many of his father's friends were poets and writers, one of them the poet Evaristo Carriego, who used to arrive at Borges' home and give dramatic recitals of his poetry. Borges would later recall: "I didn't understand any of it, but poetry was revealed to me, because I saw that words were not just a means of communication, they also contained a sort of magic." As a result, Borges soon began writing his own childish poetry.

In 1914 the Borges family set off for an extended holiday in Europe. When Europe was plunged into chaos by the outbreak of World War I in August 1914, the family remained in neutral Switzerland where Borges went to school in Geneva and enjoyed long boat rides with his sister Norah on the lake. An eager and accomplished student, he was soon fluent in German and French, and began omnivorously devouring the literature of these two countries, being particularly drawn to the musical lyrics of the German poet Heine and the lugubrious romanticism of Baudelaire. He also became especially interested in the pessimistic philosophy of the German thinker and essay writer Schopenhauer, as well as the rather more robust Anglo-Catholic writings of G. K. Chesterton. The verses Borges now wrote began to be influenced by such thinkers and poets, but this was still very much apprentice work.

After the war, in 1919, the Borges family traveled to Spain. For Argentinians of the period, Spain was regarded as the somewhat backward "mother" country—Argentina looked upon itself as very much a modern American country. Nonetheless Spain remained a thriving cultural center and at the time had developed a lively artistic avant-garde, producing artists such as Pablo Picasso and Juan Gris as well as the poet Antonio Machado and the celebrated "generation of '98." The Spanish avant-garde literary tradition was represented by the Ultraists, a Spanish version of the modernism that was now sweeping through Europe. The Spanish Ultraists rejected the earlier generation of Romantic poets as decadent, insisting upon innovation and an up-to-date view of the modern world. It was now, under the influence of Ultraism, that Borges began writing his first mature poems.

When Borges returned with his family to South America in 1921, he imported Ultraism with him, and it quickly became a major influence among the young poets of Argentina. Although Borges had by now been imbued with a deep love of European culture, his homecoming awoke an enthusiastic love for his native city. Buenos Aires was becoming a booming metropolis, complete with its own subway and new skyline of high-rise buildings. Here was a suitable setting for Borges' modern Ultraist poems, which now began appearing in local literary magazines.

In 1923 the twenty-four-year-old Borges published his first book of poems, entitled *Fervor for Buenos Aires*. It was published at his own expense (with 130 pesos given by his father), and its cover contained a woodcut illustration by his sister of the sun setting above a typical one-story house in the suburbs of Buenos Aires. The book included such poems as "Unknown Street," which contained the lines:

> Twighlight of the dove
> the Hebrews called the beginning of evening
> when the shadow does not mire the footsteps
> and the coming of night is recognized
> like an awaited music

In Spanish, these free-verse lines are particularly musical and evocative, as can be seen from the first line, which reads in the original: "*Penumbra de paloma.*"

In order to publicize his book, Borges took to secretly slipping copies into the pockets of the overcoats hanging in the office of the leading literary magazine. Some of these copies were read by the writers who owned the overcoats, a few of whom went so far as to give a favorable mention of Borges' book in print.

Despite Borges' literary sophistication and his leading role among the young poets of

Buenos Aires, the bespectacled young man seems to have been rather shy when it came to women. In the tradition of the period, his father had given him money and sent him to a brothel at the age of nineteen in Geneva, but for Borges this had apparently proved a distressing fiasco, leaving the sensitive young poet somewhat traumatized. But Borges' repressed, scholarly, rather English manner hid a passionate soul, and it was during this period that he became engaged to Concepcion Guerrero, whom he described as "a very wonderful girl of sixteen, Andalusian blood, great black eyes, and an agreeably gentle serenity with deep reserves of tenderness." The relationship was purely platonic, as was expected in such a conservative Latin society, but it did generate a number of love poems by Borges. Unfortunately it generated little else, partly because Borges still lived very uneasily with his sexuality, and partly because he was afraid to break away from his possessive mother.

During the 1920s Borges would have a number of unsatisfactory platonic love affairs. He would also continue to write poetry, publishing two more volumes which showed him developing an increasingly individual voice as well as the interests that would one day inform his finest work. The latter can be seen from titles such as "General Quiroga Rides to His Death in a Carriage," "Manuscript Found in a Book of Joseph Conrad," and "The Mythical Founding of Buenos Aires."

The first of these poems is about a leading figure in Argentinian history who played a violent role in the troubled years following independence before being murdered in 1835 on orders from the right-wing dictator Rosas. The poem ends with Quiroga's assassination, when:

> weapons without mercy swooped in a rage upon him . . .
>
> . . .
>
> Now dead, now on his feet, now immortal, now a ghost,
> he reported to the Hell marked out for him by God,
> and under his command there marched, broken and bloodless,

the souls in purgatory of his soldiers and his horses.

In the 1920s Borges also helped found a number of literary magazines; most of these were short-lived, but in 1930 he was one of the founder members of *Sur* (South), which soon established itself as the leading literary medium in South America. Borges would publish a number of his essays, poems, and short stories here, and its editorial board would include many of his closest literary cronies.

Also in 1930 Borges published a biography of the poet Evaristo Carriego, whose poetry recitals "in an exaggerated manner" had so inspired him in his childhood. Carriego had been fascinated by the characters who haunted the lowlife dives of old Palermo. As a young man he had watched the gauchos (Argentinian cowboys) who became gangsters in this wild hinterland between the city and the open countryside, the dandified crooks with their jewelry and flash suits, and the wild women they fought over. Years later Carriego had taken the shy Borges on trips into old

Palermo, pointing out to him the various characters. Carriego was dead now, but Borges' interest in the dives of Palermo remained, and here he latched on to an old knife fighter called Parades, who continued to show him around.

For years Borges had been writing fewer and fewer poems, and now, after another disastrous love affair, his poetic inspiration dried up altogether. In 1930, at age thirty-one, he once again reluctantly accompanied his mother and father to a resort hotel at Adrogué where they spent the summer months, and it was here that word reached him of the death of Parades. Borges decided to write a tribute to his old criminal friend "to record something of his voice, his anecdotes, and his particular way of telling them." The result was a short piece called "Man on Pink Corner," which is told by an anonymous hoodlum in the bordello bar on Pink Corner in Palermo. The hoodlum describes how he once saw Rosendo Juarez, who had a reputation as the toughest knife fighter in Palermo, challenged to a duel by a stranger from another district. Juarez refuses the challenge, and his mistress La Lujanera is so disgusted by his cowardice that she goes off with the stranger. The hoodlum is so ashamed by what he has witnessed that he leaves the bar. Later La Lujanera reappears in the bar; she is highly upset and tells how a man has killed her new lover in a knife fight. The hoodlum implies that it was he who killed Juarez, to restore the pride of Palermo.

Borges had found his own voice as well as his own metier. He now began to write a series of short pieces, which would be collected and published in 1935 under the title *A Universal History of Infamy*. These stories purport to be factual descriptions of minor historical characters, ranging from an eighteenth-century Japanese master of etiquette to Billy the Kid.

These narratives are in many ways influenced by the adventure stories of Robert Louis Stevenson. They make no attempt at psychological depth but are nonetheless filled with ironic twists and unexpected observations that reveal much about the fate of the characters they describe. "The Disinterested Killer Bill Harrigan" gives an oblique slant on the life of the man who would become Billy the Kid, filling in incidents from his childhood in the slums of nineteenth-century New York:

> At the age of twelve he fought in the gang of the Swamp Angels, that branch of divinities who operated among the neighborhood sewers. On nights redolent of burnt fog, they would clamber out of that foul-smelling labyrinth, trail some German sailor, do him in with a knock on the head, strip him to his underwear, and afterward sneak back to the filth of their starting place.

Such are the squalid urban origins of the great hero of the American West. Bill Harrigan, the man who will become Billy the Kid, is tempted to "Go West!" by the tawdry cowboy melodramas put on in the theatres of the Bowery. With a subtle nod to the Westerns of the future, Borges now shifts the scene: "History (which like certain film directors, proceeds by a series of abrupt images) now puts forward the image of a danger-filled saloon," and we fast-forward to one night in 1873 in a New Mexico bar in the middle of the desert.

22

Bill Harrigan, the red-topped tenement rat, stands among the drinkers. He has downed a couple of *aguardientes* and thinks of asking for one more, maybe because he hasn't a cent left.

Suddenly the bar falls silent:

Some one has come in—big, burly Mexican, with the face of an old Indian squaw. He is endowed with an immense sombrero and with a pair of six-guns at his side. In awkward English, he wishes a good evening to all the gringo sons of bitches who are drinking. Nobody takes up the challenge.

Over half a century before the advent of the spaghetti Western, Borges has picked out the satiric-realist ingredients of this subgenre which so potently evokes the legendary-historic reality. We are there; we can almost hear the plaintive twang of the music. With the minimum of deft words, Borges manages at the same time both to evoke and overcome the cliché.

Bill is told that the Mexican newcomer who has just entered the saloon is Belisario Villagran from Chihuahua. No sooner is he informed of this than Bill simply guns down the Mexican from behind the sheltering wall of tall cowboys with whom he has been talking at the bar. He then tells them: "I'm Billy the Kid, from New York." Thus is the legend born. Billy the Kid has shot his first victim, in cold blood.

Billy then goes on to create his legend, carving out for himself an infamous career: "The details can never be recovered, but it is known that he was credited with up to twenty-one killings— 'not counting Mexicans.'" Finally, after seven desperate reckless years, one hot July night he rides down the main street of Fort Sumner:

> The heat was oppressive and the lamps had not been lighted; Sheriff Garrett, seated on a porch on a rocking chair, drew his revolver and sent a bullet through the Kid's belly. The horse kept on; the rider tumbled into the dust of the road.

All night long Billy the Kid lies in the dust howling and blaspheming in his death agony, until finally he dies next day:

24

He was shaved, sheathed in ready-made clothes, and displayed to awe and ridicule in the window of Fort Sumner's biggest store.

Other exotic characters in *A Universal History of Infamy* include a Chinese woman pirate who consults the night stars to discover her fate, the imposter Tom Castro whose unexpected success leads to disaster with a fairy-tale ending, and Hakim of Merv, the mysterious prophet of Islam whose unveiling leads to a hideous discovery. These stories, and their central characters, are supported by an edifice of facts, some esoteric, some legendary, some banal—all seemingly historic. Fact merges into fiction or imagined event to form an exotic but utterly plausible literary cocktail. The vignettes of events take on legendary status, yet these minor characters on the fringes of history become, in the telling, very much a part of the universal history of something far greater than themselves.

In 1937 Borges' sixty-four-year-old father suffered a stroke which paralyzed the left side of his body. This event seems to have prompted the thirty-seven-year-old Borges to strike out on his own and attempt, for the first time in his life, to earn a living. His previous paid work had consisted of occasional essays and film and book reviews for various magazines, all of which had paid a pittance, ensuring that he continued living at home with his parents. For the first half of his life, all he had ever been was a middle-class literary playboy, living largely among others whose financial existence was similarly cushioned. Only his vast scholarship, the result of his continuing wide reading, and his gradually emerging talent, marked him out as any different from his mostly mediocre friends.

As one would expect, the shortsighted, middle-aged, and inexperienced Borges had some difficulty in finding paid employment in Buenos Aires, whose previously buoyant economy was now beginning to suffer from the worldwide Great Depression of the 1930s. Eventually he managed to find an ill-paid post in the Miguel Cané municipal library, which happened to be named after one of his ancestors. The library was on the other side of town from his parents' home, in the working-class district of Almagro Sur, and getting there involved a long tram journey to the end of the line, followed by a long walk. When Borges arrived all he had to do was catalog books for an hour or so, whereupon he was free to read. His colleagues were a boisterous lot, who spent their time talking about football, girls, and fights, and his reserved bookish manner just didn't fit; no one else was interested in the actual books in the library. Borges was soon plunged into despair by his first real contact with a working existence: "Sometimes in the evening, as I walked the ten blocks to the tramline, my eyes would be filled with tears [at] my menial and dismal existence."

He also knew that he was a failure in his father's eyes—a timid, unmarried, middle-aged writer who still lived at home and had published only a few largely unread works of poetry and short stories. This was an opinion that Borges would never have the chance to remedy, for his father died in 1938. Borges would continue to work in the library for another nine miserable years, but this period would see his transformation from a writer of promise into one of major achievement.

The year 1938 would also bring a further crushing blow for Borges. For some years now, his eyesight had been growing weaker, and on Christmas Eve he went to collect a woman with whom he had fallen in love, in order to take her home to dinner with his mother. The elevator was out of order, and as he was late he decided to run up the dim stairway, where a recently painted window which opened inward had been left open to let the paint dry. Borges would later recall what happened next, ascribing the experience to a character in his story "The South":

> He hurriedly took the stairs. Something in the dimness brushed his forehead—a bat? A bird? On the face of the woman who opened the door to him, he saw an expression of horror, and the hand he passed over his forehead came back red with blood.

Owing to his bad eyesight he had not seen the large pane of glass across the stairs. The result was a number of severe cuts to his head and neck;

28

these became infected, and within a week he was suffering from serious blood poisoning. As he lay in bed he developed a high fever and began suffering from hallucinations; soon he was on the point of death. For several days he could no longer speak, and in his delirium he believed he had gone mad. Fortunately he managed to survive this crisis, but as he recovered he began to worry that his mind had suffered permanent damage and that he might be left mentally defective.

When he was able to get up, Borges was overcome by a sensation of the preciousness of his existence and experienced an overwhelming need to express himself in a manner that was utterly his own. As a result, he felt freed from the tyranny of his endless reading, which had caused him to base his writing on quasi-factual events and characters from history. From now on, he decided, he would invent his own history, making use of esoteric fragments from what he had read. Instead of being ruled by history, he would create it; instead of relying upon the past, he would reinvent it and venture into a timeless world of his own making.

As early as 1936 Borges had written a spoof review of a nonexistent book, "the first detective story written by a native of Bombay city," which he had published under a pseudonym. Now he decided to write an ingenious story in a similar vein, which would be called "Pierre Menard, Author of Don Quixote." It is narrated by a rather pompous literary critic from Nîmes in the south of France, who has been looking through the papers left by the obscure French writer Pierre Menard. The critic even goes so far as to list, in chronological order, Menard's few publications, along with their publication dates and such magazines as they have appeared in. These works are a cunning blend of reality and imagination—the magazines cited are real enough, and the subjects treated are real enough. The works include "a monograph on Leibniz' *Characteristica universalis* (Nîmes 1904)" and "a transposition into alexandrines of Paul Valéry's *Cimetière marin* N.R.F., January 1928)." The latter futile exercise of turning Valéry's great poem into another metrical form, which was alleged to have appeared in the (real and highly prestigious) *Nouvelle Re-*

*vue Francaise,* gives a hint of what is to come. But as Borges' narrator-critic then emphasizes, this list of publications includes only Menard's *visible* works.

> I shall turn now to the other, the subterranean, the interminably heroic production . . . that must remain . . . unfinished. This work, perhaps the most significant writing of our time, consists of the ninth and thirty-eighth chapters of Part I of *Don Quixote.* . . . I know that on the face of it such a claim is absurd; justifying that "absurdity" shall be the primary object of this note.

Borges' critic now goes on to explain how Menard had wanted to write a contemporary version of *Don Quixote.* In preparation for this he had begun by trying to immerse himself totally in the seventeenth-century Spanish world of the work's author, Cervantes, to the point where he can *be* Cervantes. But he soon realized that this was impossible; so instead he decided to attempt the difficult task of "continuing to be Pierre Menard and coming to the Quixote *through the experiences of Pierre Menard.*" In this way he would be able to reproduce a faithful version of *Don Quixote,* yet written by himself. This Menard managed to do so well that what he writes is word for word the same as the original. But here the critic comes into his own: "The Cervantes text and the Menard text are verbally identical, but the second is almost infinitely richer." The critic even goes on to quote a passage from Cervantes and the corresponding passage by Menard. These are of course precisely the same. But, as the critic argues:

> The contrast in styles is equally striking. The archaic style of Menard—who is, in addition, not a native speaker of the language in which he writes—is somewhat affected. Not so the style of his precursor, who employs the Spanish of his time with complete naturalness.

Borges' story is of course a literary hoax, which depends on a rather weak joke. Yet in Borges' telling, the joke assumes its own plausibility and becomes full of resonance. Borges is well aware that at least part of this joke is at his own expense. Any writer who relies upon past literature for his inspiration is in a way guilty of plagiarism. But then, isn't all literature now plagiarism of sorts? At this late stage in the development of literature, is originality really possible? Hasn't everything been tried before? What more is there to say? What new styles are left to invent? At the same time as implying these questions, Borges hints that our knowledge of the author of a work, our knowledge of who he is and what he has done, in some subtle way influences how we read his or her work. Suppose the wild precocious poetry of the vagabond Rimbaud had in fact been written by a retired bank clerk living out his fantasies? What if the half-blind Borges had been found to have written the works of Hemingway? What if the works of Renoir had been produced by an autistic child? Such suggestions slyly undermine all confidence in our interpretation of a work of art *judged purely on its own merits*. These are just a few of the implications in what may appear at first as a rather dry-as-dust literary joke, resting on an implausible suggestion about *Don Quixote*.

Borges had managed to free himself from the tyranny of fact by reproducing a fact (word for word!). Next he attempted an even more imaginative flight from the restrictions of reality and actual history. "Tlön, Uqbar, Orbis Tertius" is also, in its own way, a colossal literary hoax. This piece is told in the first person, this time as if by Borges himself. It begins by describing how one evening he was talking after dinner with the Argentinian writer Bioy Casares (an actual friend of Borges), who happened to mention a country called Uqbar. Borges had not heard of this country, and eventually they track down a description of it in an obscure pirated edition of *The Anglo-American Cyclopedia*. Here Uqbar is described in such a way that it appears to be somewhere in the Middle East, though where precisely is not clear.

Borges then tells how two years later he comes across a mysterious single volume of a reference work: *A First Encyclopedia of Tlön (Vol. XI, Hlaer to Jangr)*.

I now held in my hands a vast and systematic fragment of the entire history of an unknown planet, with its architectures and its playing cards, the horror of its mythologies and the murmur of its tongues, its emperors and its seas, its minerals and its birds and fishes, its algebra and its fire, its theological and metaphysical controversies—all joined, articulated, coherent, and with no visible doctrinal purpose or hint of parody.

Having set himself the task, Borges now embarks upon a convincing description of this curious world, which in many ways appears to be a parallel world to our own, or perhaps a distorted mirror-image of our thought. The language of Tlön has no nouns, and its people thus have no conception of objects persisting in time and space. Its science is without causality and consists largely of psychology. Its mathematics is even more perplexing.

The basis of Tlön's arithmetic is the notion of indefinite numbers; it stresses the importance of the concepts "greater than" and "less than," which our own mathematicians represent with the symbols > and <. The people of

Tlön are taught that the act of counting modifies the amount counted, turning the indefinites into definites.

Borges describes a world that appears to be much like the philosophy of the Irishman Berkeley, who famously believed "esse est percipi"—that things only exist when they are perceived. On Tlön, an archaeologist can simply think of an ancient artifact for it to exist. Yet this Berkeleyan world is curiously permeated with Plato's concept of idealism—in which pure ideas are the only reality, the world being made of an impure mixture of such ideas. There are also many cunning references, both explicit and implicit, to other philosophers—such as Hume, Schopenhauer, and Russell, each of whose ideas have their place in this artificial world.

As one would expect, this re-creation comes into its own with Borges' description of the literature of Tlön, which is very much a sly parody of elements of his own writing. Here on Tlön every work is created by a single author who exists beyond time and is anonymous. Thus there can be

no such thing as individual creation or even plagiarism. Despite this:

> Literary criticism often invents authors: It
> will take two dissimilar works—the *Tao Te
> Ching* and the *1001 Nights*, for instance—
> attribute them to a single author, and then in
> all good conscience determine the psychology
> of that most interesting *homme de lettres*.

The description of this planet, which consists
of a blend of Berkeleyan and Platonic philosophy, comes to an end as follows:

> Things duplicate themselves on Tlön; they
> also tend to grow vague or "sketchy," and to
> lose detail when they begin to be forgotten.
> The classic example is the doorway that con-
> tinued to exist so long as a certain beggar fre-
> quented it, but which was lost to sight when
> he died. Sometimes a few birds, a horse, have
> saved the ruins of an amphitheatre.

Beneath these lines is written, almost as if in
defiance, "Salto Oriental 1940"—the real time
and the real place (in Uruguay) where Borges

(may have) completed this work. But the story now takes on a further twist, for there follows "Postscript—1947," the full import of which may escape the twenty-first-century reader—for Borges actually wrote this in 1940, and thus at the time it contained words from the future!

The postscript states boldly: "So many things have happened since 1940. . . . Allow me to reveal some of them." Borges then playfully attempts to clear up the mystery of Tlön with the hypothesis proposed by his friend Martinez Estrada: "The splendid story had begun sometime in the early seventeenth century, one night in Lucerne or London. A secret benevolent society (which numbered among its members Dalgarno and, later, George Berkeley) was born; its mission: to invent a country." But after several years of meetings and discussions, "the members of the society decided that one generation would not suffice for creating and giving full expression to a country." Each of them selected a disciple to carry on his work, and from then on that "hereditary arrangement" was continued, and two centuries later "the persecuted fraternity" crossed the Atlantic to take up residence in the New World.

Borges continues with the description of various strange events which culminate in a discovery in 1942 in a trunk shipped from Poitiers in France: "Among the pieces, trembling softly but perceptibly, like a sleeping bird, there throbbed, mysteriously, a compass." The letters on its dial were recognized as belonging to one of the alphabets of Tlön. "This was the first intrusion of the fantastic world of Tlön into the real world." Toward the end of the postscript, its author claims: "If my projections are correct, a hundred years from now someone will discover the hundred volumes of *The Second Encyclopedia of Tlön*."

"Tlön, Uqbar, Tertius Orbis" is a long piece (by Borges' standards), stretching in most editions to around thirteen pages (surely no coincidence). Some have found this a little too long and elaborate for what is essentially another literary hoax. Others have marveled at the consistency and ingenuity of Borges' elaboration of this world beyond our world, which appears to impinge upon our world. This is, among other things, a metaphor for the life of the mind, which also consists of ideas that take on life only when we conjure them up in our mind.

The world of Tlön is also, in another aspect, a metaphor for the entire history of philosophy, to which so many have contributed—even down to Borges' admission of the near futility of individual philosophers' efforts in this endeavor: "The plan is so vast that the contribution of each writer is infinitesimal." (We are reminded of the pessimistic conclusion reached by the critic in "Pierre Menard, author of Don Quixote": "There is no intellectual exercise that is not utterly pointless.") Despite this, there appears to be one fundamental guiding principle to Tlön. Midway through the first section, Borges comes to the illuminating conclusion: "It is no exaggeration to say that the classical culture of Tlön is composed of a single discipline—psychology—to which all others are subordinate." At last we have the key. But do we? All activity of the mind can be seen as subsumed under psychology!

These two pieces in Borges' new voice—"Quixote" and "Tlön"—were published in 1941 in a collection called *The Garden of Forking Paths*—named after the final story in the book, which is described by Borges in his introduction as "a detective story" (as if the others required no detective work). In this introduction he also offers a similar tongue-in-cheek explanation of why his works are so short:

> It is a laborious madness and an impoverishing one, the madness of composing vast books—setting out in five hundred pages an idea that can be perfectly related orally in five minutes. The better way to go about it is to pretend that those books already exist, and offer a summary, a commentary on them. . . . A more reasonable, more inept, and more lazy man, I have chosen to write notes on *imaginary* books.

This playful aspect of Borges' writing should be borne in mind at all times when reading his works. They may include much arcane and esoteric scholarship, but they were conceived as *jeux d'esprit*—jokes, hoaxes, games. Their more profound aspect becomes apparent only *after* one has seen the joke.

Borges had now triumphantly discovered his own literary territory, and his friends recognized that he had suddenly emerged as a major writer. *The Garden of Forking Paths* was duly entered for the 1941–1942 National Literary Prize, and to widespread astonishment in literary circles was overlooked in favor of an undistinguished work by the son of a popular Uruguayan historical novelist. Borges was not even awarded second or third prize; his book was dismissed by an official spokesman as

An exotic and decadent work which oscillates, in response to certain oblique tendencies in contemporary English literature, between the fantastic tale, boastful and recondite erudition, and the detective story—obscure to the point of darkness for whoever reads it, even the most cultivated (excluding those who might be initiated in the new magic) . . .

This convoluted insult in fact contained a coded message. The world was by now plunged into World War II, and though Argentina was theoretically neutral, its government covertly supported the Axis powers, Nazi Germany and fascist Italy. (Argentina was where many Nazis on the run from justice for war crimes would set up home after the war.) Under such circumstances, no National Prize was about to be awarded to a work with "tendencies" toward England. *Sur* immediately launched a campaign intended to rectify this insult, dedicating an entire edition to Borges' work "on the occasion of his not being awarded the National Prize for Literature."

Two years later Borges published an expanded version of his collection, for which he would coin the deftly appropriate title *Fictions*. From now on this would be the name given to Borges' most characteristic works—a new form which lay at the overlap between tales, essays, autobiography, and parody. Among the additional fictions in this volume appeared what would become Borges most unforgettable piece—ironically, a tale about someone who can never forget anything. This is called "Funes the Memorious" (or sometimes "Funes, His Memory"). The basic story is simple enough: after a riding accident, a young man from the remote Uruguayan pampas called Ireneo Funes finds that he can remember everything. The narrator, who had encountered Ireneo Funes before his accident, tells of his final visit to the nineteen-year-old, who now lies in a cot in a darkened room, smoking. The narrator, plainly Borges himself, has sat all night, listening to everything Ireneo has told him. Ireneo Funes had begun by talking about the ancient Persian king Cyrus, who was able to call every man in his vast armies by his name, then he had talked about Mithradates Eupator, who could speak all twenty-two languages spoken in his kingdom, and he had followed this by talking of other ancient figures renowned for their memory.

With obvious sincerity, Ireneo said he was amazed that such cases were thought to be amazing. He told me that before that rainy afternoon when the blue roan had bucked him off, he had been what every man was—blind, deaf, befuddled, and virtually devoid of memory.

He explained how he had lived as if in a dream, looking without seeing, hearing without listening, forgetting almost everything he experienced. But the accident had changed his life. When he came to, after falling off his horse, "the present was so rich, so clear, that it was almost unbearable, as were his oldest and even his most trivial memories." Borges manages to convey with great imaginative power what it was like for Funes, explaining that whereas we might perceive a glass of wine on a table,

> Funes perceived every grape that had been pressed into the wine and all the stalks and tendrils of its vineyard. He knew the forms of the clouds in the southern sky on the morning of April 30, 1882, and he could compare them in his memory with the veins in the marbled binding of a book he had seen only

once, or with the feathers of spray lifted by an oar on the Rio Negro on the eve of the Battle of Quebracho.

Borges' stories often hinge upon one small leap of the imagination, which must somehow be made plausible in order to convince readers and carry them into the writer's world of fantasy. This is frequently achieved with a blend of mock and actual scholarship. Sometimes it is the sparsity of his factual prose that convinces, and at other times it is the sheer felicity of his writing— the telling particularity of the images, which manage to convey an entire world. In the passage describing Funes' memories we can see what he sees, we get the gist of all that fountains continuously through his mind, the foundation of the world we barely notice. (Funes in Spanish has suggestions of fountain and foundation.)

Another of the additional fictions is particularly relevant to the contemporary preoccupation with alternative readings of biblical events. "Three Versions of Judas" is couched in the form of a short essay, rather than a story, and has all

46

the accoutrements of an article in an academic journal, including long footnotes and biblical references. The article describes how in 1904 the Swedish scholar Nils Runeberg of the University of Lund wrote a book called *Kristus och Judas* (Christ or Judas), in which he thought he had discovered "the key which unlocked one of theology's central mysteries." He argued that Judas's betrayal of Jesus Christ, which resulted in his crucifixion, was no mere provocative act, intended to goad Christ into assuming his sacred role, thus fulfilling the prophecies and God's will. Instead it was "predetermined, with its own mysterious place in the economy of redemption."

When Runeberg's book was published it was greeted with a storm of angry criticism. "Theologians of every faith brought forth refutations." As a result, Runeberg decided to rewrite the book, modifying his opinions. In doing so, he argued that Judas did not betray Christ because of greed "the basest motive . . . [but] a motive at the opposite extreme: a hyperbolic, even limitless asceticism." Runeberg goes even further, arguing that Judas "labored with titanic humility; he believed himself unworthy of being good." This blasphemous argument is backed with convincing evidence from both the Bible and consequent theological claims concerning God's intentions, before arriving at its astonishing conclusion concerning God's mysterious ways. According to Runeberg, God chose to appear on earth in the most unlikely form:

> In order to save us, He could have chosen *any* of the lives that weave the confused web of history: He could have been Alexander or Pythagoras or Rurik or Jesus; he chose an abject existence: He was Judas.

This time, when Runeberg's new revised book is published it is greeted with universal disdain and indifference, which leads him to a perceptive conclusion:

> Runeberg sensed in that ecumenical indifference an almost miraculous confirmation. God had ordered that indifference; God did not want His terrible secret spread through-

48

out the earth. Runeberg realized that the hour had not yet come.

Runeberg had committed a dark sin, and like so many who had behaved in a similar fashion he realized that he would surely be punished. Those who revealed what was meant to remain hidden, who revealed the truth before its time, were inevitably punished most severely. What "infinite punishment" would he suffer "for having discovered and revealed the terrible name of God"?

Runeberg became crazed with fear at the prospect of what would happen to him. "Drunk with sleeplessness and his dizzying dialectic, Nils Runeberg wandered the streets of Malmö, crying out for a blessing—that he be allowed to share the Inferno with the Redeemer." The article ends by recording that on March 1, 1912, Runeberg died of a ruptured aneurysm. The author adds that he will be remembered by specialists in heresy for having added to the concept of the Son the complexities of misery and evil.

But the ironic resonances of this short piece persist long after we have read its last words. It is not difficult to see in Borges' telling of the tale that Runeberg himself took on a role of betrayal perhaps as great as that of Judas, and thus he too might have been God. This is but one of the highly blasphemous interpretations that Borges insinuates. By comparison, Dan Brown's tall story of *The Da Vinci Code*, with its revelations about Judas being Christ's complicit collaborator, are no more than idle jests.

When *Fictions* was published in 1944 it was awarded the Prize of Honor by the Society of Argentine Authors. But Borges' period in the sun would be brief. In 1946 the populist-nationalist leader Juan Perón took power in Argentina and immediately set about establishing a fascist-style dictatorship. Borges, who along with his literary friends had previously signed several anti-Perónist declarations, was singled out as a leading intellectual enemy. It was decided to make an example of him, and he was dismissed from his post in the municipal library. Instead, by way of ridicule, he was "promoted" to the post of inspector of chickens and rabbits in the municipal market. (The cowardly connotations of chickens and rabbits were intended as part of the insult.) Borges turned down the position but now found himself without a job. Fortunately he managed to obtain an ill-paid post as editor of a magazine, and eked out a living with literary journalism. To make matters worse, his eyesight was deteriorating badly.

Borges was now forty-six years old, sexually inexperienced, and still lived with his mother. Once again he fell in love, this time with a twenty-eight-year-old middle-class woman named Estela Canto, who worked as a secretary but longed to be an actress. They both had things in common: she too was losing her sight and lived with her mother, she also spoke English fluently and enjoyed reading. Estela recalled Borges during this period:

> Everything Borges said had a magical quality. Like a conjurer, he pulled unexpected objects out of an inexhaustible hat. . . . And they were magical because they suggested the man he really was, the man hidden behind the Georgie whom we knew, a man who, in his

shyness, was struggling to emerge, to be recognized.

Estela enjoyed spending evenings with Borges and his more bohemian literary friends. Afterward Borges would insist upon walking her back to her mother's, which involved a four-mile hike through the night streets of Buenos Aires to the southern suburbs. Borges' friend Bioy Casares offers a vivid snapshot of them starting out on these crosstown walks:

> There was Estela Canto, who was practically blind, and Borges, who was practically blind—and she was drunk most of the time. After dinner with us, on the few evenings she came to our house, out they went into the street, these two blind people . . .

It seems they usually made it to her house, but their relationship remained essentially platonic. Estela was not interested in Borges sexually, and according to her he still remained a virgin. This state of affairs would be remedied only some years later, when he had sought psychiatric help, after which he apparently had a sexual experience with a "dancer."

These were difficult political times. As the Perón quasi-fascist regime tightened its grip on the country, demonstrations rose against the government. One day Borges' seventy-two-year-old mother and his sister Norah came across one of these protests and spontaneously joined in. In the ensuing police roundup they were both arrested. Borges' mother was lucky to escape with a month's house arrest while the middle-aged Norah spent a month in prison, where she was purposely placed in the prostitutes' wing. The half-blind Borges could only sit at home fuming impotently.

For the time being such emotional and physical problems appear to have been largely sublimated by Borges into his writing, which continued as before. He was now at the height of his powers, and the stories he wrote during this period, along with the earlier *Fictions*, are generally regarded as his finest work. In 1949 he published another collection of fictions entitled *The Aleph*.

The title story of this collection opens with a telling image of how the banality of everyday life can wear away even the most precious of memories. The narrator—Borges himself, we assume—recounts how on the very day of the death of Beatriz Viterbo, the woman he had hopelessly loved, "I noticed that a new advertisment for some cigarettes (*blondes*, I believe they were) had been posted on the iron billboards of the Plaza Constitución; the fact grieved me deeply, for I realized that the vast unceasing universe was already growing away from her, and that this change was but the first in an infinite series."

Beatriz herself is described as having been "tall, fragile, very slightly stooped; in her walk, there was (if I may be pardoned the oxymoron) something of a graceful clumsiness, a *soupçon* of hesitancy" (very similar in fact to Estela Canto, to whom the story is dedicated).

Each anniversary of Beatriz's death on April 30, 1929, the narrator recounts how he called at her family home to pay his respects. In this way, on those "melancholy and vainly erotic anniversaries" he had come to know her cousin Carlos

Argentino Daneri, a refined, grey-haired man who works in a minor capacity in some obscure library on the outskirts of Buenos Aires. Carlos Argentino is a pompous man, an unpublished writer who is "full of pointless analogies and idle scruples." This is of course a deft, depreciating parody of Borges himself. But Carlos is also a portentous, verbose bore; and one anniversary, when the narrator brings along a bottle of brandy, Carlos begins to open up, launching into his damning picture of "modern man." The narrator observes, "So witless did these ideas strike me, so sweeping and pompous the way they were expressed, that I associated them immediately with literature."

"The Aleph" is filled with such sly humor, often at the author's own expense. The joke really begins to take off when Carlos mentions the vast poem he has been working on in secret for many years, called "The Earth." Carlos explains to the narrator in his characteristically pretentious manner that his poem is "centered on a description of our terraqueous orb" and will be filled with "picturesque digression and elegant apostrophe."

Carlos then proceeds to read out a stanza of what proves to be truly banal poetry; undaunted, he follows by explaining precisely how and why this stanza is "interesting from every point of view." As if this were not enough, he now reveals that his intention in "The Earth" is nothing less than "to versify the entire planet"—to describe every building, every place, every country in the entire world. By this stage, in 1941,

> He had already despatched several hectares of the state of Queensland, more than a kilometer of the course of the Ob, a gasworks north of Veracruz, the leading commercial establishments in the parish of Concepción, Maria Cambaceres de Alvear's villa on Calle Once de Septiembre in Belgrano, and a Turkish bath not far from the famed Brighton Aquarium.

Some time after this, Carlos calls the narrator one day in an agitated state. The landlord is about to demolish his family house, and this will bring about a catastrophe. Carlos confides that "he had to have the house so that he could finish the poem—because in one corner of the cellar there was an Aleph."

Carlos goes on to explain to the narrator the precise nature of an Aleph: it is "one of the points in space that contain all points . . . the place where, without admixture or confusion, all the places of the world, seen from every angle, coexist." He had originally discovered it in the cellar during his childhood; and now the Aleph is the source he is using to supply him with all the information he needs for his great poem "The Earth."

The narrator thinks Carlos has gone mad but nonetheless is intrigued and rushes to Carlos's house. Here Carlos takes him down through a trapdoor into the cellar. And here he sees the Aleph. The narrative then pauses, as the narrator (Borges) explains:

> I come now to the ineffable center of my tale; it is here that a writer's hopelessness begins. Every language is an alphabet of symbols, the employment of which assumes a past shared

by its interlocutors. How can one transmit to others the infinite Aleph?

Borges' joke now takes on a different tenor. He has announced to his readers that he will attempt to describe the indescribable, and somehow make the impossible possible. "In similar situations mystics have employed a wealth of emblems." He explains how a Persian mystic spoke of a bird that was somehow all birds, how another spoke of a sphere whose center was everywhere and whose circumference was nowhere, while the prophet Ezekiel's mystical evocation involved an angel with four faces, facing to all points of the compass at once. As a piece of writing this is at once bold, resonant, skillful, and humorous—involving facing in all these four directions at once. It is bold because although he has told you that what he is about to describe is indescribable, he dares to describe it; in so doing, his writing becomes a resonant symbol (of the ineffable, later of the entire world, and even more); and all this is achieved with superb, almost understated skill:

> Under the step, toward the right, I saw a small iridescent sphere of almost unbearable brightness. At first I thought it was spinning; then I realized that the movement was an illusion produced by the dizzying spectacles inside it.

And it is of course humorous, in that despite describing his feat as impossible he has in fact achieved it—he has managed to describe something we know does not exist. But we do want it to exist, on a number of different levels. On the literary level, we want to believe in the story so that it can continue. On a more philosophical level, we want to believe that it is at least theoretically possible to describe everything that exists: science as well as philosophy attempt to do just this, in their own different ways. This aspect of the Aleph is conveyed when Borges peers into it. Although the Aleph is only two or three centimeters in diameter, "universal space was contained inside it, with no diminution in size."

Such a thing was perhaps easily acceptable to thinkers of earlier centuries, such as the medieval mind. And there is a direct (and acknowledged) reference in Borges' story to Blake's "to see heaven in a grain of sand." But apart from historic and literary reference, how can a modern mind accept such a thing as an Aleph? Borges manages to convince us by his skillful choice of words, which have an air of scientific sobriety and exactitude— for the modern mind is indeed attuned to accepting such an image. This is very much how we are used to conceiving of the atomic world, where each individual atom may be viewed as a minute solar system. The spinning electrons and the nucleus take up but an infinitesimal part of the whole, the rest of which can well be seen as a "universal space . . . contained inside it."

The Aleph is small, yet within it there is room for an all but infinite cornucopia of images, as we see when Borges peers into it:

I saw the populous sea, saw dawn and dusk, saw the multitudes of the Americas, saw a silvery spider-web at the center of a black pyramid . . . saw in a rear courtyard on Calle

Soler the same tiles I'd seen twenty years before in the entryway of a house in Fray Ben-
tos, clusters of grapes, snow, tobacco . . . saw
a woman in Inverness whom I shall never forget, saw her violent hair, her haughty body,
saw a cancer in her breast . . .

This is God's eye. It is also the memory of Funes
the Memorious. And it is the world viewed "sub
specie aeternitatis" (under the gaze of eternity)
which Spinoza describes in his pantheistic philosophy. It is everything and at the same time our
potential for seeing everything: the ambition of
science, history, and philosophy, even psychology. It is human aspiration to know the truth.
And in Borges' words it is simultaneously beau-
tiful, wondrous, and somehow overwhelming.
We believe it—as we believe in the possibility of
such all-seeing vision—at the same time as we
know it is impossible for us to achieve. It is both
possible and impossible, just as in Borges' fiction
it both exists and yet cannot exist.

The story of "The Aleph" unfolds in a number of twists, which range from the philosophical

to the autobiographical, with Borges the humorist never far below the surface. This is certainly one of his finest pieces, on more levels than may be found in the in-joke and the literary hoax. The main story purports to have been written in 1941, and ends with Borges emerging from the house containing the Aleph into the everyday world of the Buenos Aires streets. Borges the narrator has treated Carlos as if he has suffered a nervous breakdown, and has advised him to go to the country to recover. There follows a postscript, seemingly written two years later in 1943. This tells how, six months after the demolition of Carlos's house, his epic poem was published to great acclaim. Borges even goes on to describe how it came second in the National Prize for Literature, adding, "incredibly, my own work *The Sharper's Cards* did not win a single vote."

Having published "The Earth," Carlos is now busy at work on another epic, "his happy pen (belabored no longer by the Aleph) has been consecrated to setting the compendia of Dr. Acevedo Diaz to verse." Diaz was in fact the winner of the National Prize for Literature in the year that Borges' *The Garden of Forking Paths* was purposely disregarded. It would seem to be a suitably Dantean punishment for the vain and pompous Carlos to spend his energies reducing the leaden prose of Diaz to even more leaden verse.

The narrator discusses the Aleph: the irony being that the narrator began by doubting whether such a thing could exist while Carlos, who once needed it to help him produce "The Earth," no longer requires it to help him produce his poetry. Instead of an all-seeing Aleph, he now has as his inspiration a paltry work whose artistic inspiration matches his own. Borges goes on to discuss both the nature and name of the Aleph: "In the Kabbala that letter signifies the En Soph, the pure and unlimited godhead." Borges suggests that when Carlos named the Aleph he must have made a mistake, choosing a name from "one of the innumerable texts revealed to him by the Aleph." The narrator Borges mischievously suggests that this must therefore have been a false Aleph (in his jealousy apparently overlooking the detail that Carlos had in fact seen these texts, thus making it a real Aleph!). The narrator then produces a beautifully involved spoof argument to support his claim of falsehood, in which he discusses a real Aleph. This has never been seen (and thus its miraculous powers have never actually been observed) because it lies inside one of the stone pillars surrounding the central courtyard of the Amr mosque in Cairo, one of the holy places of Islam. The story ends with a plea that is both realistic and metaphorical, resonant and piercingly wistful:

> Does that Aleph exist, within the heart of a stone? Did I see it when I saw all things, and then forget it? Our minds are permeable to forgetfulness; I myself am distorting and losing, through the tragic erosion of the years, the features of Beatriz.

> *For Estela Canto*

Thus the story comes full circle, both for Borges in the story and for Borges in real life.

Several of the pieces in the collection *The Aleph* bear resemblances to one another, or to other earlier pieces, and one even refers directly to another: the brief "The Two Kings in the Two Labyrinths" is intended as the story that is referred to in the preceding "Ibn-Hakam al-Bokhari, Murdered in His Labyrinth." From the look of it, Borges' imagination was beginning to fail him—a curious state of affairs for one whose inspiration drew upon such a vast and seemingly inexhaustible range of sources. The overuse of labyrinths, and the image of the labyrinth, now become a repetitive feature in his work. This may in part have been a side effect of his failing sight—under such circumstances daily life must have been very similar to attempting to negotiate one's way through a labyrinth. Another recurring image is that of the miraculous quasi-talismanic object, such as the Aleph itself, and the Zahir (a coin that had metaphysical qualities). And it is now that we begin to notice how much libraries crop up again and again, either as themselves or as images. In *Fictions*, "The Library of Babel" begins with the line: "The universe (which others call the Library) is composed of an indefinite, per-haps infinite number of hexagonal galleries." This image of the universe as a library may well be how Borges was reduced to seeing things in his limited reality, but such an artistic vision becomes oppressive, especially when these fictions are so short and rely so much upon bookish references. Here we notice also Borges' use of the word *infinite*, which along with that cliché of ambiguity the mirror, crops up with dulling frequency in Borges' works. But in mitigation it must be said that his repetitive use of these images and themes—often as mere props—did lead to a re-finement and deepening of his fictions. Their very presence seemed to inspire Borges to improved in-sights, so that the earlier versions which he later repeats may be seen as rehearsals. As for instance with "Funes the Memorious," where Funes' all-inclusive memory is a marvelous metaphor, but there is no doubt that its repetition—in varied form—in "The Aleph" leads to an even more profoundly resonant idea.

The story "Emma Zunz," which appears in *The Aleph*, is perhaps a conscious attempt to break free from such constricting literary territory. Unusually, the protagonist here is a woman. Not so unusually, Borges uses a story that is not original—but instead of taking his plot from a literary, mythological, or historical source, he takes it from a story told to him by his friend Cecilia Ingenieros. She was another woman with whom Borges fell in love around this time, and the fact that she was a dancer suggests that she might have been the very dancer with whom he was said to have first had a complete and satisfactory sexual relation. Even so, she soon broke off their "engagement," but like so many other women Borges had known she remained his friend. Borges could certainly be charming and delightful company for a woman, even if the glow of sexual attraction shone somewhat dimly in this near-blind magician of the word.

Indicatively, the plot of "Emma Zunz" hinges on a sexual act. Perhaps more psychologically significant is the fact that it is a brutal sexual act, and one perpetrated on a woman who simultaneously invites it upon herself yet views it with distaste. Borges' use of "himself" as a narrator in many of his stories, as well as his endlessly suggestive literary technique, and the fact that many of these stories contain hidden references and in-jokes for his friends, certainly encourages such psychological readings of his works. And Borges was aware of this. As early as his creation of Pierre Menard, he had covertly endorsed this manner of interpreting works of literature.

Previously Borges had only referred to the sexual act, almost in passing; but in "Emma Zunz" he becomes more open about this subject, even offering an insight into its effect: "All men, in the vertiginous moment of coitus, are the same men." Several other features make this an uncharacteristic piece, lacking as it does the usual plethora of literary references and scholarly allusions, with just a fleeting reference to mirrors and only a suggestion of a labyrinth. The story is simple and simply told but nonetheless hinges on a deception. The father of Emma Zunz had been wrongly accused of embezzlement at the mill where he worked, causing him to flee the country; some years later he committed suicide. Before leaving, he had revealed to his daughter that the real culprit was Aaron Loewenthal, who was then the manager of the mill but has now risen to become one of its owners. Emma still works at the mill, and when she hears of her father's wretched death far away in Brazil, she decides to wreak revenge upon Loewenthal. She arranges to meet him—but immediately before this meeting she goes down to the docks, where she pretends to be a prostitute and purposely offers herself to an unattractive foul-mouthed sailor "so that there might be no mitigation of the purity of the horror." The sailor remains anonymous:

> The man—a Swede or Finn—did not speak Spanish; he was an instrument for Emma, as she was for him—but she was used for pleasure, while he was used for justice.

The two of them pass through a veritable (but unnamed) labyrinth:

> The man led her to a door and then down a gloomy entryway and then to a tortuous stairway and then into a vestibule (with lozenges identical to those of the house in

Lanús) and then down a hallway and then to a door that closed behind them.

The sexual act between them takes place "outside time, in [a] welter of disjointed and horrible sensations." This distancing effect appears to be both a literary device, necessary for the psychology of Emma, as well as a personal device necessary for the psychology of the author (who is not indicated as a first-person narrator; this story is told in the third person). Afterward, when the sailor has gone, Emma tears up the money he has left her. "Sadness and revulsion hung on Emma like chains."

Emma now goes to her meeting with Loewenthal, at his home above the mill. Things do not go quite the way Emma had planned, but in the end she shoots him with the revolver he keeps in his desk, then phones the police, claiming he has raped her and she has shot him. The final paragraph concludes:

The story was unbelievable, yes—and yet it convinced everyone, because in substance it was true. Emma Zunz's tone of voice was

70

real, her shame was real, her hatred was real. The outrage that had been done to her was real, as well; all that was false were the circumstances, the time, and one or two proper names.

Although this story may be uncharacteristic in many ways, its ironies are certainly Borgesian.

Borges dedicated one of the other stories in *The Aleph*, "The Immortal," to Cecilia Ingenieros. This too is one of Borges' finest, despite its lapse into labyrinths and the old fading-memory ploy. The twists of its plot are too complex for satisfactory summary but make for a classic adventure-mystery story which transcends time and has all the trappings of a Borgesian scholarly caper with its footnotes and spurious claims. At the same time it is occasionally deeply evocative, especially when the Immortal himself tells us:

On October 4, 1921, the *Patna*, which was taking me to Bombay, ran aground in a harbor on the Eritrean coast. I disembarked; there came to my mind other mornings, long in the past, when I had also looked out over the Red Sea—when I was a Roman tribune, and fever and magic and inactivity consumed the soldiers.

This story sometimes has the puzzling effect of rousing in us nostalgia for a life that we could not possibly have lived. Such irony would certainly not have escaped its dedicatee.

Two years after the publication of *The Aleph*, a French translation of *Fictions* appeared, the first of Borges' works to appear abroad. In 1953 Perón was finally ousted and a military government installed in Argentina. Two years later Borges was appointed head of the National Library. By now he was too blind to read, a paradox worthy of one of his stories, and he could not refrain from remarking how he had been given "at one time 800,000 books and darkness." This position had previously been held by no less than two blind Argentinian writers—José Marmol and one of Borges' literary heroes, Paul Groussac. Borges marked this coincidence with "Poem of the Gifts," in which the writers blend in their blindness:

. . . God, who with such splendid irony
granted me books and blindness at one
touch . . .

Groussac or Borges, now I look upon
this dear world losing shape, fading away
into a pale uncertain ash-grey

From this time on, Borges would dictate his poems to secretaries at the National Library. The physical act of writing was no longer possible for him, and his stories, essays, and journalistic pieces were dictated at home to his aging mother. Worst of all, on medical advice he was now forbidden to read. This meant he had to rely upon readers as well as those who took dictation. As his existence had been narrowed by his fading sight, gradually he had learned to invest his entire life into the acts of reading and writing—now even this independence had been taken from him. All he had left was his mind.

Borges continued to write poetry throughout his long literary career. Indeed, he would claim, "First and foremost, I think of myself as a reader, then as a poet, then as a prose writer." But by this stage in his career, his poetry had been eclipsed—in quality at least—by his prose. The subject matter of his poems remained similar to that of his fictions, as can be judged from even a random selection of their titles: "Spinoza," "Matthew XXV, 30," "Conjectural Poem," "The Labyrinth," and so forth. The following are typical lines, taken from "Everness":

> One thing does not exist: Oblivion.
> God saves the metal and he saves the dross,
> And his prophetic memory guards from loss
> The moons to come, and those of evenings gone.

Sometimes his poems appear as if they are trial runs for his fictions. Significantly, the poetic impulse never deserted Borges, and this is all too evident in his prose works, which usually retain a poetic quality. The poet's eye constantly raises these fictions above their often dry and scholarly subject matter.

For Borges, the rewards of fame now began flowing in. A year after his appointment to the National Library, he was installed as professor of

English literature at the University of Buenos
Aires and awarded the National Prize for Literature. But he continued to work, publishing essays, poetry, and fictions in magazines. In 1960
he published a major collection of prose and
verse called *The Maker* (often translated as
*Dreamtigers*).

In his Foreword, Borges describes arriving in
the morning at his new workplace:

> *The sounds of the plaza fall behind, and I en-
> ter the Library. Almost physically, I can feel
> the gravitation of the books, the serene at-
> mosphere of orderliness, time magically
> mounted and preserved. To left and right, ab-
> sorbed in their waking dream, rows of read-
> ers' momentary profiles in the light of the
> "scholarly lamps" as a Miltonian displace-
> ment of adjectives would have it.*

As ever with Borges, such serenity is seldom un-
marred. This Foreword is addressed to the poet
Leopoldo Lugones, one of his predecessors in
this office, with whom Borges had had an am-
bivalent relationship. Lugones had been the

leading representative of the Symbolists, the generation that the Ultraists sought to overthrow. Borges and his young cronies had published jibes against Lugones, but Borges could not help retaining a certain regard for the skill and artistry of Lugones' poetry. As he continues in his Foreword, addressing Lugones:

> *These reflections bring me to the door of your office. I go inside. We exchange a few conventional, cordial words, and I give you this book. Unless I am mistaken, you didn't dislike me, Lugones. . . . At this point my dream begins to fade and melt away, like water in water . . . you, Lugones, killed yourself in early '38.*

*The Maker* is not without its labyrinths, mirrors, and reliance upon dreams, while the fictions are now even shorter (averaging around a page in length). They tend to be more literary in flavor. But there is no denying that this collection contains many fine fictions and a number of excellent short conceits. One of the latter is "On the Exactitude of Science," which covers less than half a page and purports to be from an ancient learned volume. It tells of an empire where the art of cartography reached perfection, the map of the empire eventually becoming so large and exact that it matched the reality it described "point for point." But the following generations were not so enamored of this map, seeing it as pointless, and decided to get rid of it:

> They delivered it up to the Inclemencies of Sun and Winters. In the Deserts of the West, still today, there are Tattered Ruins of that Map, inhabited by Animals and Beggars; in the Land there is no other Relic of the Disciplines of Geography.

Two pieces in *The Maker* have Dantean subject matter, a perennial favorite with Borges. The first of these, "Paradiso XXXI, 108," is a not wholly successful reworking of old Borgean themes; but it does contain the thought-provoking lines: "A Jew's profile in the subway might be the profile of Christ; the hands that give us back change at a ticket booth may mirror those that soldiers nailed one day to the cross."

The second Dantean piece, "Inferno I, 32," is a delightful double conceit of compact eloquence which remains in the mind long after one has read its three hundred or so words. We see the captive leopard who is to inspire the image in the first book of Dante's *Inferno*. Its animal nature, and its repression, are cunningly evoked, as is the secret of its raison d'être, which God tells it in a dream: "*You shall live and die in this prison, so that a man I have foreknowledge of may see you a certain number of times and never forget you.*"

The second paragraph shows the other side of this example of God's will. In lines of astonishing simplicity and poetic power, Borges elaborates his conceit:

Years later, Dante was to die in Ravenna, as unjustified and alone as any other man. In a dream, God told him the secret purpose of his life and work; Dante, astonished, learned at last who he was and what he was, and he blessed the bitterness of his life. Legend has it that when he awoke he sensed that he had received and lost an infinite thing . . .

This passage neatly encapsulates the strength and conviction of Borges' vision, but also its flaw. He rightly points out how at his death Dante must have felt "as unjustified and alone as any other man." Amidst the uncertainties of our existence we can know nothing of our fate. Whether we believe in such a thing, whether we believe in God or not, such knowledge remains beyond us. Even with faith we cannot escape from our feelings of human failing, ultimate solitariness, and lack of justification for our lives. Yet Borges, in this piece and so many others, purports to see the world from above all this. Everything is fated, determined, part of God's purpose. We may derive comfort from this—and Borges' vision encourages us to do so—but we cannot live with this knowledge, we do not live with this knowledge, amidst the everyday hurly-burly, suffering and joy of the accidental world we inhabit. Borges' vision is comforting because it is inhuman; like Spinoza he wishes to see the world under the gaze of eternity. But Spinoza only claimed that this was how the world existed in his philosophy. He did indeed aspire to live in this knowledge, but he knew that this was an aspiration, perhaps fleetingly attained in moments of illumination but not lived during every hour of every day. You cannot experience, or describe, a complete and particular life, or world, from this point of view—except perhaps in short, poetic fictions. Any longer, any more particular and realistic, and the vision could not be maintained. Its very determinism, its very generality, its lack of free will and accident, would make it feel hopelessly wooden. Ultimately, and tellingly, it would appear *inhuman* and *lifeless*. Fortunately Borges' skill and art manage for the most part to disguise this fact, and we are granted—momentarily—a satisfying, even enlightening, view of how the world *might* be. But this is, ultimately, nothing but a comforting illusion.

This said, *The Maker* also includes a seminal piece called "Borges and I," where he examines the relationship between himself and his writing persona. Instead of viewing this under the gaze of eternity, he chooses to view it with the eyes of psychology, and the result is a truly tantalizing piece which provokes all manner of questions about how we live our lives. Significantly, it is questions we are provided with here, rather than answers.

A year after the publication of *The Maker*, Borges and Samuel Beckett were jointly awarded the internationally prestigious French Prix Formentor for 1961. Within a few months two collections of Borges' work appeared in English. The Prix Formentor meant he was now assured translation into many languages, and his period of worldwide fame and recognition dates from this period. In the same year Borges taught for a semester at the University of Texas, and in the following years he frequently traveled abroad, giving lectures and receiving honorary degrees. He was accompanied on these trips by his mother Leonor, who was now in her mid-eighties. She remained an upright, fashionably attired lady; by contrast Borges wore loose-fitting suits which hung about his corpulent body, his hair was greying, and his blind face looked aged in repose. Leonor and Borges were often mistaken for man and wife.

Borges was now able to visit many of the places he had only read about; and everywhere he went seemed to have literary associations, particularly Britain. As he wrote:

> I made many pilgrimages: to London, so teeming with literary memories; to Lichfield and Dr. Johnson; to Manchester and De Quincey; to Rye and Henry James. . . . I visited my grandmother's birthplace in Hanley, one of the Five Towns—Arnold Bennett country.

His literary heroes haunted the streets and houses, often more alive to him than the people who now lived in them. He also visited Madrid and Geneva, which he had last seen some forty years earlier. "Geneva is a city I know better than Buenos Aires," he claimed, and in a way this was true. With his faded eyesight, he now actually *saw* practically nothing. Geneva he had last seen when his eyes were clear; for years he had walked the streets of Buenos Aires as if in a mist.

These trips soon began to exhaust Leonor, and after 1963 she was no longer able to accompany Borges abroad. Younger women were all too eager to escort the famous old man around the world, and perhaps inevitably there was now a recurrence of Borges' old emotional problems. He began falling in love with women who had become friends, were enchanted by his company, but felt no physical attraction for him. Fortunately this time the problem had a happy resolution, when Borges encountered Elsa Astete, whom he had last met when she was seventeen. Borges had fallen in love with the young Elsa and had written her a number of love letters, but she had married someone else. Meeting her again was like fate. Elsa was now a fifty-seven-year-old widow, and once again he fell in love with her. She was willing to make an independent home for Borges, the one thing he now wanted more than anything else. At last, the sixty-eight-year-old Borges had found his soul mate. In 1967 he and Elsa were married. Even his mother seemed to approve.

Borges' travels abroad may have brought him the reassurance of fame, but they also exposed him to increasingly persistent questioning on one of the few topics he really knew nothing about—politics. This was the sixties: American campuses were in an uproar over the Vietnam War, in May 1968 Paris was virtually taken over by a student uprising, and Latin American politics was in a ferment following Castro's left-wing revolution in Cuba. On Borges' tours of Latin American countries, he found himself being asked questions which, in his naiveté, he thought he could answer in his own idiosyncratic fashion:

> I believe in revolution, and am waiting for it to come. In the revolution there will be no political leaders. There will be no propaganda, there will be no banners and there will be no flags. . . . When they tell me about some new revolution I always ask "and do they have a flag?" and when they say "yes," I know that it is not my revolution.

Such answers were at best inadequate and served only to alienate his young politicized campus audiences. The students were largely of the left, a view Borges did not share, for all his claim to believe in revolution. Borges was in fact conservative in so many ways—in his life, in his appearance (he always wore a suit and tie), in his tastes, and in his routine daily existence. The "revolution" he believed in was a purely intellectual concept. And he genuinely thought stability was the best answer for Argentina, even if this meant a measure of repression. Meanwhile Latin American politics was becoming violent: violent repression was being met with violent demonstrations. The simplicity (and difficulties) of the increasingly polarized situation were best summed up by the great Chilean poet Pablo Neruda, a Communist: "There were only two ways, in South America—either you supported the fascists, or you became a communist." It is worth remembering that during this period Nelson Mandela, Sartre, Picasso, and many other well-known figures were professed Communists or believed in armed revolution. Communism was anathema to Borges, though he certainly didn't believe in fascism, either. And unlike so many left-wing writers of the period, Borges had actually suffered for his anti-fascist beliefs, losing his job and having his mother arrested (and worse was to come).

In 1970 Borges published another collection of fictions entitled *Brodie's Report*. In the Foreword he attempted once more to explain his political convictions:

> I have joined the Conservative Party (which act is a form of skepticism), and no one has ever called me a communist, a nationalist, an anti-semite, or a supporter of Hormiga Negra [a previous bandit leader] or of Rosas [a previous military dictator]. I believe that in time we will have reached the point where we will deserve to be free of government. I have never hidden my opinions, even through the difficult years.

The eleven pieces collected in *Brodie's Report* are distinctly different from those in *Fictions, The Aleph*, and *The Maker*. According to Borges, these were "new ventures into straightforward storytelling," and in the process of writing them he returned to the locales of several of his earliest stories—the rough-and-ready districts on the outskirts of old Buenos Aires and outlying regions. Here the realism is often historical and violent, as for instance in "The Encounter," which tells of "the once-famous much-discussed case of Maneco Uriante and a man called Duncan." The story takes place in 1910, "the year of the comet and the Centennial," and the protagonists are now both dead. All who witnessed the event took a solemn oath never to tell what they had seen, and "I too raised my hand to swear . . . with all the romantic seriousness of my nine or ten years." The subject matter harks back to that of "Man on Pink Corner," but with a metaphysical twist. Despite this, it has the same gripping realism as Borges' early brutal tales of infamy, and the knife fighting is all too vividly evoked:

> As their forearms (with no ponchos wrapped around them) blocked the thrusts, their sleeves, soon cut to ribbons, grew darker and darker with their blood.

Yet the twist in the tale is classic Borges, who tells how all those present saw "the body sprawled beneath the sky—but what they saw was the end of another, older story." It was this "older story" that had caused the witnesses to swear an oath of silence, and that prompts the narrator to conclude: "Things last longer than men."

"The Intruder" is also about knife fighters, this time the two brothers Cristián and Eduardo, who fall in love with the same woman. This brutal story dates from before Borges' marriage, and was in fact dictated to his mother. She is said to have disliked the story intensely, but, according to Borges, when he became stuck at the end of the story it was his mother who provided him with the words, spoken by one of the brothers, that would bring the story to its conclusion. Unknown to the reader, Cristián has taken a drastic step, which is revealed in his last words to his brother as he stops their ox cart on a lonely backroad at dusk:

> "Let's go to work, brother. The buzzards'll come in to clean up after us. I killed 'er today. We'll leave 'er here, her and her fancy clothes. She won't cause any more hurt."
> Almost weeping, they embraced.

Rather than fall out with his brother, Cristián has been willing to murder the woman they both love. Such was the ending provided by Borges' mother.

This story is of course deeply linked to Borges' relationship with his mother, and the feelings of betrayal he would experience whenever he fell in love with another woman. The brutal words supplied by his mother only serve to reinforce this link. Nothing was to be allowed to come between their familial love for each other.

Even after Borges' marriage, this epic Oedipal saga of Leonor and her son continued. By 1970 Borges' marriage to Elsa had broken down irretrievably. They had nothing in common, and, as his friends pointed out about their "fated" meeting after all those years, "fate" happens only in books. On July 7, 1970, Borges simply walked out of the home he had set up with Elsa, never to return.

In 1973 the Perónists swept back into power in Argentina. Borges was abroad at the time but sent word home that he was resigning from his post as director of the National Library. He would now spend most of his time out of the country. But he did make a number of unguarded remarks in public about the situation in Argentina, and he would pay for these when he returned home. Isabel Perón, who had replaced Eva ("Evita") as Perón's wife, had now taken over the country after his death. In an interview with *Newsweek*, Borges referred to Isabel Perón as "a poor substitute for Eva. A streetwalker too. The first one died, poor thing, so they said we'll have to find a replacement. Streetwalkers are easy to replace." After this Borges' mother, now in her nineties, received death threats over the phone, and a bomb was placed outside the building in Buenos Aires where Borges was living, though it failed to explode.

After the collapse of Borges' marriage he had once again returned to live in the family home with his mother. But Leonor was now extremely old and infirm, little more than a presence in a bed. A skeletal figure, descending into pain, she began to long to die, and finally did so on July 8, 1975, at the age of ninety-nine.

In 1975 Borges published another collection of thirteen short works, entitled *The Book of Sand*.

This marked a return to his fictions and was greeted with acclaim, with forty thousand copies being sold within two months of publication—a huge figure in Argentina for a purely literary work. None of his previous works had achieved such popularity.

The opening piece in *The Book of Sand* is entitled "The Other," and is similar in subject to the piece "Borges and I," which he had written some fifteen years earlier. The contrast between the two pieces is revealing. In "The Other" we find Borges sitting on a bench beside the Charles River in Cambridge, north of Boston, on a cold February day. Large chunks of ice are floating down the grey river, and this reminds him of the ancient Greek philosopher Heraclitus, who believed that all is flux, and said, "No man steps into the same river twice." A man sits down at the other end of the bench and begins trying to whistle what turns out to be an old Argentinian tune. Borges describes how "the tune carried me back to a patio that no longer exists and to the memory of Alvaro Melián Lafinur, who died so many years ago." The man turns out to be a younger version of Borges himself, who is sitting on a bench beside the River Rhone in Geneva.

So far so good. But the piece now descends into a somewhat trite discussion about what lies in the future for the younger Borges, and which one of the two is dreaming the other. This discussion extends over several pages (overly long for Borges) and soon begins to drag. The two figures are brought together by a single idea, which unlike so many of Borges' best pieces has little resonance beyond itself. It is just an idea, a metaphysical whim almost, which seems to tell us almost nothing about Borges himself, the other younger figure, or the human condition that it strains to illuminate. It reaches toward but never manages to grasp its potential. His earlier pieces could fill the reader with wonder as one followed Borges' twists and turns, being afforded glimpses of deep metaphorical resonance. Yet this time there is nothing but the rather feeble overused idea of one person dreaming another into existence. In the end "The Other" is not philosophy, psychology, or even good storytelling.

Other titles hint at the decline in Borges' powers: "The Mirror and the Mask," "A Weary Man's Utopia," and so forth. In several of these pieces he is tired, both physically and creatively; it is almost as if he is just going through the motions, producing the sort of pieces his admirers would expect him to produce. For anyone else this would be quite an interesting collection, but Borges had undercut himself by producing works that far outshone the merely interesting. Only the short (three-page) "Ulrikke" hints at something new, though even this is at times overlaid with an excess of literary reference. Sometimes, however, it works: "It was at this point that I looked at her. A line somewhere in William Blake talks about girls of soft silver or furious gold, but in Ulrikke there was both gold and softness." And occasionally there is a flash of the old wit:

> Ulrikke invited me to share her table. She told me she liked to go out walking alone.
>
> I remembered an old quip of Schopenhauer's.

"I do too. We can go out alone together," I said.

And in the end, he finds love. Borges describes how he mounts the stairs and follows Ulrikke into her room (which has the inevitable mirror):

> Ulrikke had already undressed. She called me by my true name, Javier. I sensed that the snow was coming down harder. Now there was no more furniture, no more mirrors. . . . Ancient in the dimness flowed love, and for the first and last time, I possessed the image of Ulrikke.

Once again Borges had fallen in love. When he traveled abroad he was now accompanied by his young secretary, Maria Kodama, who was more than forty years younger than he. This time Borges was wary of hurting himself, and it was some time before he revealed his feelings. By this time Maria appears to have been well aware of what was happening, and to have welcomed Borges' attention. She agreed to become his wife—but there was one serious snag. Divorce was illegal in Argentina, and this seemed an insurmountable problem while Borges still lived in his home country. But in the early 1980s he learned that he had cancer of the liver and did not have long to live. In 1985 he left Buenos Aires forever to take up residence in the one city of which he always had fond memories, from his schooldays to his many subsequent visits: Geneva. ("The Other" may have lacked in art, but it contained its element of the old Borges magic in its hint of prophecy: he would end up as the figure he had dreamed of, sitting by the river in Geneva.)

In April 1986 Borges married Maria Kodama, making use of a series of truly Borgesian subterfuges. The marriage took place in a remote provincial registry office in Paraguay, which astonishingly required neither of them to be present—a truly metaphysical union which was presumably made possible by an all too physical requirement of solid cash: a conjunction that echoed the best of Borges' work. A further twist is added by the fact that the Paraguayan consulate in Geneva had no record of this event, which according to law should have been registered there. Another Borgesian twist would be added later, when the Argentinian authorities sought to annul this union but could not do so because there was no evidence of the marriage to be annulled!

Two months after Borges' elusive marriage, he succumbed to cancer and died in Geneva at the age of eighty-six, his forty-year-old bride Maria at his side.

# Afterword

In his own inimitable way, Borges had the last word on Borges. Over a quarter-century before he died, Borges had written the autobiographical piece "Borges and I." At the time it appeared as a piece of enigmatic psychology, in which he contrasted his living self ("I") with his writing self ("Borges").

> My taste runs to hourglasses, maps, seventeenth-century typefaces, etymologies, the taste of coffee, and the prose of Robert Louis Stevenson; Borges shares those preferences, but in a vain sort of way that turns them into the accoutrements of an actor.

The "I" who lives and the "Borges" who writes share so much, but in the last analysis they are separate creatures. One uses the other, and yet the other also in some ways relies upon the one.

It would be an exaggeration to say that our relationship is hostile—I live, I allow myself to live, so that Borges can spin out his literature, and that literature is my justification.

Yet the "I" who lives knows that eventually he will be defeated by the Borges who "spins out his literature." Enigmatic as ever, Borges ends with a classic stinging jest: "I am not sure which of us it is that's writing this page."

This may at first sight seem to be the self-regarding writer disappearing up his own psyche. A moment's self-examination by the reader reveals that the situation Borges has described is in fact part of the universal human condition. It is an important insight into how we all live our lives. We each of us have a living "I" and a "Borges"—a persona—who "spins out" his public self, his actions, what he does, his creations, what he "makes" of his life. The living "I" merely lives at the heart of this web we spin out of ourselves, to ensnare or keep at bay or enthrall others.

After Borges' death, passages in this piece would take on further levels of meaning, as he surely knew they would. In "Borges and I" he had written presciently: "I am doomed—utterly and inevitably—to oblivion, and fleeting moments will be all of me that survives in that other man." In life, as in death, the living Borges was all too well aware of his fate:

> Spinoza believed that all things wished to go on being what they are—stone wishes eternally to be stone, and tiger, to be tiger. I shall endure in Borges, not in myself.

# Borges' Chief Works in English Translation

*Fervor for Buenos Aires* (poems, 1921)[†]
*Moon Across the Way* (poems, 1925)
*San Martin Notebook* (poems, 1929)[†]
*A Universal History of Infamy* (short stories, 1935)[*][†]
*The Garden of Forking Paths* (fictions, 1941)[*][†]
*Fictions* (fictions, 1944)[*][†]
*The Aleph* (fictions, 1949)[*][†]
*The Maker* [*Dreamtigers*] (fictions, 1960)[*][†]

[*]major works
[†]discussed in text

*Selected Poems* (poetry, 1969)[†]
*Brodie's Report* (stories, 1970)[*][†]
*The Book of Sand* (fictions, 1975)[†]

# Chronology of
# Borges' Life and Times

1899    Jorge Luis Borges born August 24 at 840
        Tucman Street, Buenos Aires, son of Jorge
        Gullermo Borges and Leonor Acevedo de
        Borges.

1914    Borges family departs for extended stay in
        Europe. Outbreak of World War I. Borges
        attends lyceé in Geneva, Switzerland,
        where he learns French and German.

1918    End of World War I. Borges travels with
        family to Spain, where they take up
        residence. Meets members of the Ultraist
        group and publishes first poems in
        magazines.

1921    Borges family returns to Argentina to live in Buenos Aires. Borges introduces Ultraism to Argentina, publishes first book of poems, *Fervor for Buenos Aires*.

1925    Borges publishes second book of poems, *Moon Across the Way*.

1929    Borges publishes third book of poems, *San Martin Notebook*, which wins second place in Buenos Aires Library Prize; uses prize money to buy a copy of *Encyclopedia Britannica*. Wall Street crash followed by worldwide Great Depression of 1930s.

1935    Borges publishes *A Universal History of Infamy*, his first collection of stories.

1937    Borges' father suffers stroke and dies. Begins working as a cataloger in Cané Municipal Library in working-class suburb of Buenos Aires.

1938    Runs into a window, suffers blood poisoning, and almost dies. After many weeks in hospital, begins writing first characteristic fictions.

1939    Outbreak of World War II in Europe. Argentina officially neutral in conflict, but government makes no secret of its favoring the Axis of Nazi Germany and fascist Italy. December: German pocket battleship *Graf Spee* scuttled off Montevideo.

1941    Publishes *The Garden of Forking Paths,* which is widely recognized as a masterpiece.

1942    *The Garden of Forking Paths* refused the National Literary Prize for political reasons. *Sur* publishes edition devoted to Borges as protest against his failure to win National Literary Prize.

1944    Publishes *Fictions,* which includes *The Garden of Forking Paths* and new fictions.

1946    Populist Juan Perón becomes president of Argentina and establishes right-wing dictatorship. Borges dismissed from his library job and insultingly "promoted" to inspector of chickens and rabbits at local market, a job which he refuses.

1949    Publishes *The Aleph, a* collection of fictions.

1951    A French translation of *Fictions* is
        published in Paris, the first foreign edition
        of his work.

1952    Death of Eva Perón.

1953    Perónist government overthrown; Perón
        flees to Spain.

1955    Borges appointed director of the National
        Library; becomes almost totally blind.

1959    Castro siezes power in Cuba.

1960    Borges publishes collection of prose and
        verse, *The Maker* (often translated as
        *Dreamtigers*).

1961    Borges shares with Samuel Beckett the
        prestigious French Prix Formentor,
        marking the start of his international fame
        and recognition. Teaches for a semester at
        University of Texas.

1968    At the age of sixty-eight, Borges marries
        Elsa Astete Millán.

1970    End of marriage to Elsa. Publication of
        collection of short stories, *Brodie's Report*.

1973    Perónists return to power; Borges retires
        as director of National Library.

1975    Death of Borges' mother, aged ninety-nine. Publication of collection of fictions, *The Book of Sand.*

1981    Gabriel García Márquez receives Nobel Prize, thus effectively putting an end to Borges' hopes for this award.

1985    Borges leaves Buenos Aires for the last time.

1986    In April, marries Maria Kodama. June 14, Borges dies in Geneva, where he is now buried.

# Recommended Reading

Harold Bloom, ed., *Jorge Luis Borges* (Modern Critical Views) (Chelsea House, 2000). A wide range of essays on aspects of Borges' writing, ranging from "Kabbalistic traits" to "the idea of Utopia." Borges' writing invites all kinds of arcane interpretation, and it is well worth sampling the essays in this book in order to launch oneself on one's own explorations. The critics featured in this volume include Ronald J. Christ, professor of English at Rutgers University, and Emir Rodriguez-Monegal, a renowned Borges scholar—all edited by the legendary Harold Bloom, who was professor of humanities at Yale.

Jorge Luis Borges, *Collected Fictions*, trans. by Andrew Hurley (Penguin, 1999). This is the best compendium of Borges' imaginative prose works (several translations of many of his works are available). This book includes Borges' own preface and some forty pages of highly informative notes "intended only to supply information that a Latin American . . . reader would have and that would color or determine his or her reading of the stories."

Jorge Luis Borges, *Selected Poems* (Penguin, 2000). This well-chosen selection by Alexander Coleman covers the majority of Borges' career and includes all his finest work in this genre. It also includes thirty pages of illuminating notes. Borges' poetry is as wide-ranging and liable to esoteric reference as his prose.

Evelyn Fishburn and Psiche Hughes, *A Dictionary of Borges* (London 1989). This fascinating work ranges from Abbasids (the Islamic dynasty) through Hung Lu Meng (a seventeenth-century Chinese text) to the purely fictional Zur Linde. It is filled with nuggets of information, all of which are relevant to Borges' texts (with references supplied). Ideal for browsing and starting up fresh topics of inquiry, which will return you to Borges with renewed enthusiasm.

Emir Rodriguez Monegal and Alastair Reid, eds., *Borges: A Reader* (Plume, 1981). This 360-page selection covers the whole of Borges' works rendered into English by a number of different translators. This includes poems and essays, journalistic pieces and reviews, as well as stories and fictions. Many of the shorter prose pieces are unobtainable anywhere else in English and make fascinating reading, especially those on Joyce, Kafka, and Virginia Woolf, all of whom proved instrumental to Borges in the creation of his unique style.

Martin S. Stabb, *Jorge Luis Borges* (St. Martin's, 1975). A less daunting critical work in Twayne's World Authors Series, which treats different aspects of Borges' life, works, and reception by his critics. The book places Borges in context and contains all manner of illuminating quotes, insights into the stories, and fascinating interpretations. There is also a good short section on Borges' life and times.

Edwin Williamson, *Borges: A Life* (Penguin, 2005). This 570-page work is the latest in a long line of biographies and memoirs, and claims to be the first in any language to cover the entire span of Borges' life and work. It draws on several previously untapped sources and is particularly good on how Borges' personal life influenced his writing. Edwin Williamson is professor of Spanish at Oxford University and is rated by no less than leading South American author Maria Vargas Llosa as "one of the best critics of Latin American literature."

# Index

# A NOTE ON THE AUTHOR

Paul Strathern has lectured in philosophy and mathematics and now lives and writes in London. He is the author of the enormously successful series Philosophers in 90 Minutes. A Somerset Maugham Prize winner, he is also the author of books on history and travel, as well as five novels. His articles have appeared in a great many publications, including the *Observer* (London) and the *Irish Times*.

Paul Strathern's 90 Minutes series in philosophy, also published by Ivan R. Dee, includes individual books on Thomas Aquinas, Aristotle, St. Augustine, Berkeley, Confucius, Derrida, Descartes, Dewey, Foucault, Hegel, Heidegger, Hume, Kant, Kierkegaard, Leibniz, Locke, Machiavelli, Marx, J. S. Mill, Nietzsche, Plato, Rousseau, Bertrand Russell, Sartre, Schopenhauer, Socrates, Spinoza, and Wittgenstein.